D1734979

The Law of Attraction

How I Activated
The Law of Attraction

And Manifested Everything I Wanted, using a Spiritual Light

David Ashworth

First published by David Ashworth, 2022,
Whitchurch, Shropshire.

ISBN 978-0-9559067-9-4

Books by David Ashworth:

*Dancing with the Devil as you Channel in the Light – Survival for
Healers and Therapists*
The Keys of Transformation – Birth of a New Light
VISION
Golden Rabbit (autobiography)
Ocean of Emotion
The Yellow Kite
Fairy Stories – Encounters with Nature Spirits
The Princess and the Bear (poetry)

The Vision Journey (movie)
The Shaman's Journey – A Guided Meditation (CD)
Revealing Truth (DVD) (From a live workshop)

dave@davidashworth.com
www.Law-of-Attraction.guru

CONTENTS

There is only one thing
that prevents anyone aligning with

The Law of Attraction…

Creating a
Vibrational Shift in Consciousness!

You can study
The Law of Attraction
for a thousand years,
but if you can't create a
Vibrational Shift in your Consciousness,
you won't get anywhere!

Or as Rumi said:

"Whoever enters the way without a guide,
Will take a hundred years to travel
a two-day journey"

In this book,

I will share with you
The simple but profound Spiritual Light
that brought me into
harmony with the Universal Laws.

How it raised my vibration…

How it brought me my heart's desires…

How it created my wealth…

How it brought my life into
a place of paradise!

INTRODUCTION

This book is not about teaching you the Law of Attraction. There are many teachers out there who have written good books and have a clear understanding of the science of it. You can go and read those books and learn their techniques for yourself.

This book is about sharing with you two things:

How I did it!
and
Where you can access the Spiritual Light that helped me!

This Light continually raised my vibration, changing my life for the better and attracting everything I desired.

So, let's not beat about the bush. Time is short and you want to know the answers as to,

How the Law of Attraction works for me.

This book is only a small part of my story to help you see how my life unfolded as I aligned with the harmony of the Universal Laws.

Life Before I Attracted the Light

I was a very unlucky person in life. I worked extremely hard but never really seemed to get anywhere. Lots of people noticed how unlucky I was and said so.

Then it all began to change in my late 30s when I attracted something into my life that led me on a different path. I didn't practice the Law of Attraction. It came to me without even looking for it. I didn't even realise that I had been attracting all the things I ever wanted until one day, when I was shown, in a flash of blazing insight, how I had achieved it.

As this blazing insight filled my heart with joy, I was given the opportunity to share with you the knowledge of this simple Spiritual Light and how it took me on this incredible journey to success. As I walked this path and followed the guidance of the Light, I helped many others to transform their lives too.

Anyone, anywhere in the world can use this same Spiritual Light to achieve success. I have actually been trying to share it with people since 2005, when I first attracted it. It is a Light that illuminates your heart. There is a register on my website of everyone who ever requested a connection to the Light, numbering in the thousands.

First of all, I will share with you what happened on the day I was shown that I had attracted everything that I had ever wanted without realising it. I hadn't noticed what was happening around me because my life was focused in a different direction. I wasn't trying to attract wealth, or anything else for that matter. I was just helping humanity by sharing my Light with those who were seeking healing, support, spiritual growth and illumination of their consciousness. That is what my life is all about.

Secondly, I will share with you something of my journey, so that you know a little about me and the things I have experienced and accomplished.

Finally, I will show you where and how to access the Light that aligned me with the Law of Attraction.

This is deliberately a short book, so don't bother skipping to the end, otherwise you won't get the lesson that goes with the Light. Just sit down and read it and you will see that if the Light can do it for me, then it can do it for you.

With Love and Blessings,

David Ashworth.
March 20th 2023, Spring Equinox, Shropshire.

PART 1

HOW IT ALL CAME ABOUT

The Universe is actually trying to help
you to open the door to
everything you desire.

1 – In the Beginning

When I began writing this book, I'd never studied the Law of Attraction, although I do work with the Universal Laws every day and understand them. It's not so much about understanding the Laws intellectually, it is about living them in your heart.

I came to my understanding of Universal Laws *via* my own journey along a spiritual path rather than a mind centred or business-oriented focus. After a spiritual awakening that began in the late 1980s my life was totally transformed from running a small business servicing advertising and printing to being a hands-on healer. That was only the beginning of the most amazing life that would unfold over the following 30 years.

Having been a spiritual teacher for many years, I arrived at this point of sharing my knowledge with you about the Law of Attraction as the result of a dramatic event one day in October 2021. I experienced a massive vibrational shift that revealed how I had attracted everything that I really loved without even noticing that I was doing it. I certainly wasn't practicing any Law of Attraction teachings.

Activating the Law of Attraction is a process. It is not something you step into from the perspective of desperation, struggle, fear or indeed, wanting money. It is a journey of many ways that bring you into a place of alignment, wisdom, harmony and enlightenment. Each step helps you to see the world differently and especially how it all works behind the illusion of what we think is reality. We are all essentially playing a part in a great game but we weren't given the rule book when we arrived here.

Universal Consciousness, like all things, is both simple and complex at the same time with a great deal of subtlety thrown in for good measure. Understanding the nature of opening it up for yourself is fascinating if not frustrating, even difficult and painful at times, as we learn the rules or lessons of the game. The important thing to note right from the beginning is this:

You are not alone.
The whole Universe is working with you
all of the time.
It never takes a break!

Universal Consciousness, is the whole thing. It is everything that is both out there and within us. The whole thing functions based on Laws, Universal Laws. The Law of Attraction is only one aspect of the whole. It is important to note that all Laws are influenced by and connected to each other. Therefore, we don't attract, activate or align with just one Law because you can't isolate just one Law. You aim for the bigger picture and then each Law begins to work for you in turn.

I hope that sharing my journey of how I attracted, not just my heart's desires, but an unbelievable life too, will hearten you to try the way that was revealed to me by the Universe itself. I am sure that you won't believe some of it, but I am indeed excited to share it with you. Sharing this illuminating process never ceases to uplift me as I see others benefitting and blossoming into lives they could never have imagined.

How am I qualified to explain to you how to
Activate the Law of Attraction?

Because I did it without any knowledge
of how to do it.

Because I didn't even apply myself to the task.

I just arrived here through following the truth
in my own heart and a spiritual path.

I was guided to succeed by
the Universe itself.

2 – Astonishing Insight

I hadn't really joined up all the dots of my journey into the Law of Attraction until that day I experienced the astonishing flash of insight.

This happened when walking out of my garage late one afternoon. When closing the door, it was as if my body was gently turned around by some unseen force and I found myself looking back at two classic cars that were worth a lot of money – I mean a serious amount of money! A sum of money that I could never have found if I had to buy these cars!

The image of them hit me in the heart with such incredible joy and surprise that my feet almost came off the ground. At the same time, I heard myself say out loud, 'How did that happen? Where did they come from? It was a moment of illumination that felt like I was somehow seeing them for the first time, like they had just appeared. I was definitely seeing them in a 'new Light.'

Illumination

It all started earlier that day, the 19th October 2021. I had spoken with some colleagues who were having some major difficulties in life. After our call I continued to ponder their situation, looking for answers as to why so many things were going wrong for them. This is essentially what I do for a living. I help people solve life's difficulties from a spiritual perspective.

After lunch, I flicked on my phone to check for messages when one of those 'YouTube Shorts' popped open, all by itself. It was Bob

Proctor speaking about being in harmony with the Universe. The clip was about 22 seconds long and the word 'harmony' hit me in the heart with such intensity that it was clear this was what I was looking for to help my colleagues. That is how the Universe helps you. It gives you the answers, you just have to be alert to feel the energy in them. I look for an answer to help someone solve a problem and something within me attracts it.

As the light in the word opened my heart, a stream of consciousness began to flow through me and I wrote it down for them. It was such a powerful teaching full of Light and wisdom, that I shared it with my mailing list to help others. I knew this word 'harmony' was the answer they were looking for, we just had to work out what they were not in harmony with.

A Shift in Vibration

Personally, I had been waiting for a new direction in life to arrive since December 2016. I knew it was coming but I had no idea what it might be. Over the following days I had so much Light in my system that I was almost on fire. I knew from experience that this was a massive vibrational shift and it had been triggered by that word harmony. You can work as hard as you like on yourself but until the vibrational shift comes, as a result of your heart being filled with Light, then you can't move forward in any new direction without some measure of struggle. When you are in harmony with your life-path or what you desire, then everything flows.

Universal Consciousness is always trying to help us find our direction, or find the answers we seek, so when a YouTube clip suddenly opens on your phone and Bob Proctor gives you the answer you are looking for, then that is no accident. That is a clear example of how Universal Consciousness helps you when you are in alignment, or in 'harmony' with the Laws. The trouble is, most people would ignore such an event and write it off as some sort of weird happening. But when you have worked with the Universe for as long as I have, then you look deeper into things because there is always some guidance trying to help you.

After I closed the garage door that afternoon, a whole stream of life's events came flooding back to me. The Universe showed me how I had attracted everything I truly loved and it was all given without any effort at all. I thought about the cars again and realised that although I had invested a little money in them, the cars had really arrived by themselves. I had been guided into finding them and they had mostly been given or traded in some way or other. They had usually arrived in bits and pieces or needing some work. I had rescued, restored and rebuilt them, eventually turning them into something quite valuable. Rescuing things has always been a passion for me. Making something better than it was brings me joy. I guess my life's work is really about rescuing souls, helping people to align with their true selves through bringing Light into their hearts.

The essence of this car journey though was that there was no struggle. The cars had literally manifested. Each car had its own story to tell in the way it came to me. I found that if I chased after a car, it didn't come. I had to wait and when the time was right, the Universe would offer one.

Over the following weeks, my insights gathered pace as the Light continued to increase within me and I went through many vibrational shifts. I was taken on an inner journey of reflecting on how I had attracted everything that I truly desired, including my cottage that is set in my own personal paradise, which may not be the same as your paradise, of course.

My 10-year Plan

It is important to share with you this car journey, as this is the real key to explain my success with the Law of Attraction.

The car journey began when I was 60 years old. I sat down at my desk one day and said to myself, 'How long have I got left in life? I might have ten good years, who knows? So, what is the thing I love most that I can engage in that will bring me joy for these next ten years?'

From being a child, I had always had a passion for old British sports cars. I had owned quite a few over the years, but then marriage, work and children happen and the cars had drifted away from me.

Starting from Scratch

In the summer of my 58th year, I was driving alone up the west coast of the Lake District in my Jeep Cherokee, (something I had attracted). It was a glorious day and I suddenly realised that I had lost my mind. Or, more to the point, I had lost my heart! I thought, 'What am I doing driving this tin can when I could have the sun on my face and the wind in my hair, driving something that feeds my passion?' A few weeks later, I had found a little bright orange Triumph Spitfire. It didn't cost very much money, as I didn't have much money to spend. It was my learning curve back into old cars and I loved it.

The Spitfire really sparked my passion for the cars I had owned in the past and as I approached my 60th birthday, I set about looking for something to upgrade to. To cut a long story short, when I set my 10-year plan in motion, I had no garage and my Spitfire sat outside under a cover in winter. Not ideal for an old car.

When I was closing the garage door on that October afternoon, it was just 3 weeks before my 70th birthday. The Universe was showing me that my 10-year plan was coming to completion. In that time I had manifested a very well-equipped garage with, not only the two classic cars that I mentioned previously, but five! One of them a very rare car that I had desired since my teens. I recall in my early 20s looking at a second hand one on a garage forecourt in north Manchester and the salesman came out and said, 'Don't look at what you can't afford!' Isn't it funny how certain things stick in your mind?

The Law of Attraction is based on love.

Glancing back into the garage that day and feeling that incredible joy hit me in the heart was the Universe saying to me, 'Look at what you attracted from the moment you set your intent and followed your passion. Now you are qualified to share with people how you did it.'

In that same moment, I knew that I didn't need the cars. There was no attachment to them but as long as the love for them is there, then all is well.

If I had needed to find the money to buy these cars, they would never have arrived because the sums of money would have been way beyond my means. But on that afternoon, the Universe showed me that they arrived because I was so much in harmony with what I wanted to experience.

The wealth though, is not in the monetary value of the cars. The wealth is in the love that they bring to me as a reflection of the love that flows from my heart towards them. They bathe me in love because they were all attracted through love. When you truly love something, then you will attract it.

If your life is evolving,
then it is constantly going through
a process of change and rebirth.

Nothing can stop it except yourself!

3 – Changing my Life

This journey of understanding the Law of Attraction began for me a long time ago. In the late 1980s, I was working as a typesetter in my own business in Manchester, England. I had a wife and soon we would have two small children. I was living the same kind of life as many other people. Getting up in the morning, going to work, earning a living and working on the house at weekends. Work wasn't easy but I was quite successful with it in a small way.

Around 38 years of age, things started to become a struggle. I was working longer hours and my business was actually going backwards. I was earning less and less no matter how hard I worked. One day I sat down at my desk and said to myself. 'I'm not going to move from here until I have some answers as to what is going wrong.'

At the time, I also ran another small business supplying organic hair products to professional hairdressing salons. It was a trailblazing product that was quite a bit ahead of the curve, but because of this, a lot of people weren't really ready to take a chance on it. I had recently introduced the products to a very large salon in the south of England and I recalled that one of the staff members was an astrologer. So, I wondered if astrology had any answers for me?

I contacted the woman and asked her could she produce an astrological chart for me. After some weeks it arrived, 54 pages of hand written detail. It was fascinating because it told two stories. The first story was the me that I know and understand. The other story, according to the chart, was a person who possessed the most incredible spiritual and intuitive abilities. This second person was a total stranger to me. As far as I was concerned, I didn't have any spiritual abilities whatsoever. I reasoned though, that if the first person in this astrological story was so accurate, there must be some truth to the second person.

Starting Life Over or Rebirth

As I studied the chart over the coming months, strange things were happening to me. It was like I was being filled with some kind of energy. Some days I was being blown up physically like a balloon and becoming light headed. At times I felt like I was losing my mind. One day, I was buttering some toast in the kitchen at home when I suddenly realised that I was standing across the room watching myself buttering the toast! That out of body experience was quite alarming and was a turning point. I had to find someone to talk to that knew what was happening to me.

The energy continued to build up day by day and I was having thoughts that my life was completely on the wrong track. At the same time, I seemed to be having a breakdown, which of course, is the beginning of a breakthrough! My heart was bursting and I was hiding my tears most of the time. Tears were flowing constantly for no apparent reason, other than I felt that my heart was breaking, which it was. It was breaking open! I had this overwhelming feeling that I needed to be free. This became a recurring theme and at certain points in my life I have had to walk away from the things I created. Stepping into the void and just trusting the Universe.

When we struggle or things are not working out for us, then clearly, we are not in harmony with our life mission. We are not going in the right direction or honouring our life-path. Any difficulty that comes to us is presented by the Universe to help us see that something in our life needs attention. Difficulty is always an opportunity to see things differently. Sometimes the difficulty stops you in your tracks. When this happens, it is usually the Universe saying to you.

This has gone on long enough. You need to address your life and make changes.

There was no choice.
I had to walk away from everything in life.

Finding Courage

Change was being thrust upon me as energy and Light were poured into me. There was no choice. I had to walk away from everything in life. I had to leave my home, my wife, my children. The first night I slept for a while in a van in a service area on a motorway, until it got too cold and I went to my brother's house and slept there on the floor. I never went home again.

The Light began showing me that I had made a lot of choices that were to please other people or because others thought it was the right thing to do, or indeed because I was not strong enough to follow my own truth, even if I knew what that was. In fact, I had never really known what I wanted to do in life, I had just drifted from one situation to another as opportunities arose to work at something or other. Yet I had almost always worked for myself from being a teenager, probably because I was unemployable, lol.

Change begins with the first step and this doesn't have to be as big a step that I had to take. For most people it is just about acknowledging that something needs to change and then moving towards the change by making small adjustments. It begins with a realisation that you are not happy at some level and then addressing that unhappiness or disharmony by taking a small step. It is just about moving in the direction that the Universe is trying to guide you. As my awakening took hold though, my own first step was huge. I had to find incredible courage to change everything in my life. That first step of telling my family that I was leaving was so difficult and painful. I just knew in my heart that I had to go. I had to step off the cliff and allow myself to fall into oblivion.

I realised that the collective consciousness of

humanity was living in a box that it didn't

know how to get out of!

4 – My Healing Journey

There is something within us all that needs healing. I don't mean something painful like a broken arm or leg, but there are things hidden deeply in our consciousness that have been buried for a long time. Things we have buried ourselves or have become buried through the passage of time over many previous lives. We are a bottomless pit of life experiences, many of which have never been resolved. The lack of resolution of the things that have hurt and troubled us over time causes us to have to work very hard sometimes to overcome things that we don't really understand. Some of us are forced onto a healing path through circumstances to resolve some of life's difficulties. Others are pushed onto a healing path for reasons that may be way beyond their understanding in the beginning, but become clearer later on. Whichever it may be, we can find that we are working through the pains of patterns that continually hold us back.

As my personal chaos unfolded, I had no idea where I was going. I only knew that I wasn't living my inner truth. I really was stepping into oblivion with no plan and no direction. I abandoned myself to whatever was filling me with energy and Light, whilst at the same time the astrologer was guiding me in how to feel the truth in my heart. I didn't understand it at the time but I was being opened up by the Universe and taught how to become aligned with it.

As you pass through an awakening, everything must be broken down in order to be rebuilt. For some, it can be a totally overwhelming process and you have nowhere to go and nothing to be because you are in a process of dissolution. Your consciousness and sense of reality dissolves so that it can receive an upgrade; a new programme; a new direction. It took me three years to pass through this phase. The first year was breaking down, the second year was stabilising myself along the bottom and the third year was the phoenix-like rising into my new self.

As those three years progressed, my life totally transformed. I still ran the typesetting and hair product businesses as a kind of part time thing that just brought in enough money to sustain the family that I had left behind. I had eventually gone to live with my mother, which was a challenge in itself in my late 30s. The only thing you can think of, is that you are a total failure yet there was also an excitement in the air as new things unfolded. With hindsight, I know this was a major vibrational shift in my life, but whilst you are passing through your first transformation, you don't really understand this and I was living from moment to moment.

New people were coming into my life and I was being shown a side of life that I never knew existed. Time and again people would tell me that I was here to be a healer. Well, nothing could have been further from my reality. I was a very practical, hands-on sort of a guy, a back-room boy, a problem solver. I was now being told that my hands were for healing others. By the end of that three-year period of breaking down and rebirth, I was indeed working full time as a healer. What a crazy transformation. You couldn't make it up in your wildest imagination.

How many of us have arrived on the wrong path in life and don't even know it? I certainly didn't know it. I had just followed my nose going from job to job, mainly working for myself and then, sometime later, I find my whole life is on a totally different trajectory using some incredible abilities that the astrologer had previously written about in my chart.

As these abilities developed, I noted that this work wasn't a struggle in the way that I had always worked so hard to achieve anything in the past. It felt very natural to me. It was like I had crossed some great divide from a world I knew and understood into a world of unlimited possibility that was expanding by the day. Some kind of power was working through me that would ultimately help thousands of people. I was totally in the flow and each day was exciting and uplifting, if not a little challenging as I learned how to use these new abilities. In retrospect, so much was flowing towards me that all I had to do was get up each day and help people. Helping people seemed to be so natural for me. Prior to this awakening, I avoided people as I preferred to work quietly on my own.

Apprenticed to the Universe
Over the following ten years I worked full time as a healer. I opened my heart each day and Light poured through me into the lives of others. I had never advertised but my practice was always full. People just came or more accurately, they were sent by some unseen source. I gave talks and workshops in how to develop spiritual abilities and was also invited onto a number of radio and tv programmes.

Each client that came was most definitely sent. Each one was my teacher in that I had to learn how to see within them to help them move through their life challenges. During this time, my inner vision had opened in the most incredible ways. I was permanently astonished as to what I could see, beyond what we might call our visible reality.

I began to see into the Light of Consciousness!

As my healing work progressed I was seeing ever deeper into people. I was guided to be able to dissolve the energies that limited a person's potential. In turn, this brought about healing on many levels for them. I reached a point where I saw energy so deeply that one day I went beyond energy and began to see into the Light of consciousness. This, in turn, gave me some realisations of how the Universe worked.

Another Major Vibrational Shift

One particular day, I was working with a client and plumbing the depths of consciousness in their heart. I could sense their issue was so deep that I had to keep pushing to find it. The Light kept saying to me, 'Let go, let go.' So rather than push I tried letting go. I kept letting go and letting go and still the Light continued to give me the same message. At one point, I thought to myself, 'If I let go any more than this, I'll die.'

I could feel that I was on the very edge of leaving my life when at that very instant, my consciousness shot right through the core of my client's heart and emerged in another universe. I seemed to be moving at the speed of light across this universe, yet I knew at some level I was still inside the heart of my client. As I continued to fly at incredible speed, I was aware of approaching yet another universe, and then I could see beyond that into endless universes. It was the most incredible expansion of my consciousness, then suddenly I was back in the room again.

I could see into endless Universes!

As my client was still unconscious on the couch, I was left breathless with awe. I was shown that our heart is so much more than we understand. It is the doorway to infinite consciousness that stretches into eternity. I realised that the collective consciousness of the whole of humanity is living in a box that it doesn't know how to get out of, in comparison to what I had just experienced. Humanity's collective consciousness holds us all prisoner within the power of its vibration, not allowing us to experience the vastness of our own potential until we can shatter those bonds that hold us. It dreams of success, but is held back because it can't expand and see beyond the limitation of its own vibration.

The experience of this heart journey expanded my consciousness to an almost alarming degree. You don't just see the images, you experience the expansion into what you are witnessing. I couldn't speak for days afterwards. Each time I tried to open my mouth to explain the journey I had taken, no words would come out. Nothing could express the magnitude of this expansion.

I became the Light that Illuminated others!

My consciousness continued to open and expand for quite some time afterwards and my work transformed fully from healing to evolutionary work. My consciousness had become a kind of key that could unlock the consciousness of others. I became a Light that illuminated the Light in others. Their own Light then guided them to their own inner truth offering them the opportunity of expanding their lives into their true potential.

It had become very clear through the years that I had been chosen by Universal Consciousness to bring new things into the world to help humanity. Day by day the Light continued raising my vibration and teaching me the most incredible processes to help others. My evolution has never stopped. Even today, I go through some incredible processes of inner change on a regular basis. Once the Light begins to awaken within you, it continues gently illuminating to the next degree and guiding you along your own individual journey.

Time to close the door and walk away.

Around the year 2000, as we went through the millennium doorway, the Light showed me how to create high vibrational essences by infusing Light into water. These then offered humanity a simple, tangible way to dissolve limiting factors in their lives. They help align you with the Light of Universal Laws, which in turn help you to feel the true destiny of your life purpose. I have personally used these Light essences almost every day since I created the first ones. Today, we even have an app where you can download the vibration of a chosen essence directly into your heart, helping you to dissolve the limitations of your life.

My healing practice was totally full for ten years until one day in September 2004. As I was putting the key in the door one morning, a gentle voice said, 'Time to close the door and walk away.'

Within two weeks, around 60 people had cancelled their appointments. My healing work was finished. The door was closed and I walked away…

…once more, over the cliff into oblivion.

Universal Consciousness
trains you through challenge.

It pushes you through your limitations
so that you can grow into a
much greater expression of your Self.

5 – Big Changes will Come

I had been on this path long enough to know that resistance is futile. The journey into Universal Consciousness is one of surrender. You just surrender and wait, whilst trying to be alert to the signs, signals and opportunities that offer you direction or a new course in life.

When you have just been laid off work by your employer, your first thought is usually, 'How am I going to earn a living?' Survival is one of our strongest fear programs as humans but to be in harmony with Universal Consciousness, you must overcome this programming and learn to trust. The next door will not open for you until you find the courage to step away from your present situation and trust that something else will be given. As my employer, Universal Consciousness, cancelled all my appointments, I didn't have a choice other than to trust. I went home with nothing to do and waited. Soon, the Light spoke up and said; 'Big changes will come in January.'

I busied myself writing and creating as I have always done. A few former clients phoned up for appointments and were told that I didn't have the practice any longer, but I could speak to them on the phone, and this seemed to work quite well. In fact, it worked very well. We didn't have Skype or Zoom in those days, so there was only the land-line. I put up a very small computer desk in the corner of the bedroom and worked from there. Past clients began to return but as new clients came forward, they were displaying different energy signatures around being held back in life. As I looked deeply into them, I could see the blockages that limited their inner development and potential. I used the Light Essences or Light Programs to dissolve these energies at a distance, without having to see them personally. I found this way of working tremendously freeing for both parties. The work could all be done in a phone call. The results were impressive.

It became very clear that my healing work was over in traditional terms, but I would continue healing through the process of unlocking the evolutionary potential of the individual. This would be by telephone consultation from then on. I soon discovered that I could work more effectively than ever at a distance. It was like I had served that first part of my apprenticeship by working directly with people, and now I worked with their consciousness remotely using Light Programs to help them bring about changes.

About a year before this huge change in my working practice, I went through a very disturbing but interesting process. At the time, I possessed incredibly sharp inner vision that allowed me to see very deeply into the human energy system, but one day when working with a client, my vision became a little foggy, just a little more difficult to find what I was being guided to look for. As the week unfolded, with each client my vision deteriorated by a very measured amount. As the following week began, I had estimated that if my vision continued to reduce at the same rate, then by Friday I would not be able to see anything at all.

My Friday afternoon client was a woman that I hadn't seen before. As she came in, even before I had introduced myself, she said, 'I'm not going to tell you anything and I want you to tell me all about my life?' No pressure then! The Universe has a great sense of humour.

This is a classic example of how Universal Consciousness trains you through challenge. It pushes you through your limitations so that you can grow into a much greater expression of yourself.

I asked the woman to lay on the couch and the Light took her into unconsciousness. I sat in my chair and went out of the body, which was always how I worked. I always came back into consciousness about a half hour before the client came round. As I was brought back, I sat with my computer on my lap and began to type in a kind of semi-conscious way. Once the session was complete, I read to her what I had written. She responded by saying something along the lines of, 'How did you know all this about me, it is totally correct.' That was a great relief, I can tell you. I didn't see her again and so that was the Universe just sending someone to bring me the lesson.

Knowing without Seeing
Everything changed after that and I developed a new kind of vision, which my guidance called 'Knowing without Seeing.' In other words, you don't need to use your inner vision any longer.

The Prime Limiting Factor to your Vibration Rising

My original vision had functioned through my chakras as they had awakened, but now I became aware that I was seeing things through my heart at a much deeper level. Yet, seeing was the wrong term, it was knowing the truth within someone. As those previous two weeks had unfolded, the Light had closed down my chakras a little at a time each day so that I was forced to find a new way to see or 'know' the key issue that prevented a person developing. As my heart opened to this new level of working, it was a revelation in how I could see the limiting issues in people.

After this, the Light taught me a very specific process to help people overcome limitation. The Light called it, 'Finding the Prime Limiting Factor' to a person's evolution. As my heart looked into the person, it connected to the truth in their heart. Their heart would then guide me to see the one single energy that prevented their vibration rising to the next level.

This new way of working was all part of the preparation for what was to come in the January that I was now waiting for.

At a certain point on the
vibrational spectrum,
you come into harmony with
the Law of Attraction.

6 – I Attract the Spiritual Light

January 2005 dawned and I waited. The days and weeks past, then in the latter days of January, a new Light hit me. When I say it hit me, I mean, I saw it coming across the room in a kind of slow motion. As my mind was trying to figure out what I was seeing, the Light hit me right in the heart but it seemed like it hit me everywhere at the same time.

The image of the Light was heart shaped, emerald green and faceted like a jewel. It was extremely clear and very distinctive. I didn't know what to make of it at first and couldn't even give it a name, even though it was obvious. As the Light unfolded within me, my vibration was rocketing skywards. This new Light began to teach me things I knew nothing about. For the following six months I hardly slept for the intensity of the Light. It brought constant teachings and as I wrote them down, I tried to figure out how this Light worked. I had always been able to see and feel the energies that I was working with, so I naturally assumed I could understand how this Light functioned.

As new clients continued to call me, I was able to apply this new Light to their issues, but often without addressing the issue itself. The Light would show me the root cause of the person's difficulty, which was often based in a fear that I could see as a dark cloud of energy within them. The Light would say, 'This energy is what holds their vibration down and prevents evolution.

It is their Prime Limiting Factor.' I was then instructed to,

'Fire an arrow of Light into the cloud of darkness
and you will dissolve it.
The Light will release them from captivity
and their vibration will rise.'
They will then be able to move forwards in life,
and attract a new reality.

The Name of the Light
The Light is called The Emerald Heart Light and it became very
clear that when people stepped into it, then it helped them to see
what needed to change in their lives in order to progress. The Light
brought about healing by dissolving the limiting energies to their
potential. By illuminating and dissolving the darker energy of the
issues that prevented their vibration from rising, they could more
easily make changes to their lives. This resultant shift in vibration
offered a real sense that they were then in the flow of life, rather
than struggling with it.

I tried to write the instructions of how to use the Light, the
rules that governed it and the guidelines in how to apply it to help
move people forwards. It took me six months of toil to figure it all
out. The moment I had it, the Light totally changed its nature and
never worked the same way again. Being a little slow to learn, I
then spent another four months figuring it all out again and the
same thing happened. The Light totally changed the way it worked.
I was more than a little frustrated and wondered what the lesson
was. Then one Monday morning after I had been away by myself
for a weekend of intense study of this Light, I entered my office
and under the desk was a little brown book by Yogananda, entitled,
The Law of Success, which, incidentally, I had never read and I have
no idea where it went to either.

The Laws of the Universe

The title hit me like a bolt from the blue. It became crystal clear that I wasn't trying to figure out the instructions, the rules or the guidelines of how the Light worked. I had been given The Laws of the Universe! The Laws were wrapped up in the Light and the Light itself worked through the laws. They were inseparable. But more than this, the reason it kept changing the way it worked was a lesson for me that I could not know this Light. Nobody could, its nature is unknowable. The Light comes to you through trust. The Light is a blessing that is bestowed upon you.

When I saw that word 'Laws', it was like the brakes were taken off and my vibration was rising once again, faster than I could cope with, or that is how it seemed. I had spent almost a year trying to figure it all out when all I needed to understand was that the Light works through Laws and trust. This was a massive turn of events for me. I had to let go of trying to understand anything and just bring the Light into the hearts of those who wished to grow and change.

The Light is the teacher itself. It will not allow you to progress until you have a total understanding of what you have in your hands. It had held me back whilst I was trying to apply my old knowledge and experience to it, which of course didn't work because my consciousness was moving into a higher vibration where everything is different.

The Light is the Key to being in Harmony with the Universe.

As the teachings and my experience of working with the Emerald Heart Light unfolded, I began to understand that these were the Laws that govern the Evolution of Human Consciousness. The Light and the Laws were inseparable - they were one and the same. They were the key to being in harmony with the Universe and the key to set people's hearts free. Furthermore, I began to realise that I hadn't so much been given these Laws, but my consciousness had attracted them through the desire to help others. I was becoming the Light of the Laws and they were becoming my own consciousness. It was like my own consciousness and certain aspects of Universal Consciousness were merging and becoming inseparable. I was dissolving into the Light.

As I worked with the Light, lots of things suddenly made sense. Right at the beginning of my awakening, I had been forced to set myself free in order that I could be prepared to receive this Light; a Light which, in turn, sets you free. I had to take the difficult step into freedom to become worthy of a greater freedom.

As the teachings came to fruition, I formed The Emerald Heart School of Enlightenment. Students came and were taught and everything was in an incredible flow and moving very quickly.

The Emerald Heart Light taught me how the Universe works like a reward system. Everything you put in to helping humanity results in Universal Consciousness giving you more. It does that by raising your vibration, which in turn attracts new opportunities to you. Each vibrational level that you move up, you align with the harmony of ever-higher vibrations of Universal Consciousness. At a certain point on the vibrational spectrum, you come into harmony with the Law of Attraction as most people understand it today. Without knowing it, I had already passed that point and was becoming aligned with a Divine aspect of Universal Consciousness that would attract even greater opportunities to me.

This Light could free everyone
from the drudgery of lives
that are unfulfilled.

7 – New Developments

Every vibrational shift that our consciousness can pass through is always the foundation or spring board for the next phase of inner development. My own vibration has never stopped rising since my first awakening in the 1980s, and thus, my evolution towards a more enlightened state has never stopped unfolding. I have gained much understanding about my life, my previous lives and the potential of what I have in my hands. One night whilst sitting with the Light and working something out, I saw in a flash of insight how the Emerald Heart Light could change the whole of human consciousness. It could free everyone from the drudgery of lives that are unfulfilled. The insight was so intense, that I almost fell off my chair. Sometime later, I was given the plot for a film that would show the world how to do it, and not only that, the Light would radiate from the film and begin the process of illuminating anyone who watched it. I even managed at one point, *via* a friend, to get the idea onto Peter Jackson's desk in New Zealand, (the director of *Lord of the Rings*) but it wasn't ready to go anywhere yet, so it still sits on a shelf in my office.

A Light that Reveals Truth

I understood that the Emerald Heart Light is unique in the way it came through me and into the world. The thing that marked out my success with it was my level of trust. I totally trusted the Light. I allowed it to open my heart and expose my limitations so that I could see them. Trust seemed to be the limiting factor for some people who worked with it, plus their inability to be completely honest with themselves or find the courage to make the tough changes that needed to be made in order to prosper. The Emerald Heart Light shows us the truth in our hearts and it is then up to us to face those truths and overcome the limitations around them. It is just like the saying about 'taking the horse to water, but you can't make it drink.' You can offer the Light to people, but will they truly drink it into the depths of their heart and respond to what it shows them?

I am the example of what the Light can do for you. If it can do it for me, then it can do it for anyone. There is no secret, other than determination to be your true authentic self and follow your heart to the exclusion of all else. Those who really trusted the Light and the teachings grew at an incredible rate, their vibration continuing to rise, attracting opportunities to them.

Close the Door and Walk Away

Once again, I was asked to close the door and step away, but I had colleagues to leave the Emerald Heart School with. This was a new dawn for the evolution of humanity in a way, as unlike spiritual teachers of the past, once they left our world their Light left with them, it was rarely passed on. The Emerald Heart Light taught me how to seed it into the hearts of others so that they could continue bringing it into the world.

It was December 2015 when I finally stepped away and was aware that something new was yet to come. The months prior had been a horrendous process as I felt the Light being ripped out of my heart in preparation for the next part of my journey. I had put every moment of my life into developing the Emerald Heart School for the previous ten years; the teachings, events and spiritual retreats, etc. Of course, I knew that the heart must go through incredible processes to accommodate certain vibrational shifts but the feeling of failure or that I had not treated the Light with appropriate reverence and respect for it to be taken from me in such a way, left a lot of questions in my mind. I had struggled with my own self-doubt for months but the pain of loss slowly faded as I was prepared for the next step.

When we are forced to step away from something in this way, it is to break any attachment. Once you go through the vibrational shift, you can often return, but in a different capacity. It is like when I saw the cars that day in the garage in that amazing insight, at the same time I knew that I wasn't attached to them, didn't need them and they could go tomorrow, if necessary. They had served their purpose, which was to show me how I had attracted them.

Light flooded through me
to the degree that it was quite alarming

Dispelling the Darkness

The following February, I went through what was possibly the most intense of my many vibrational shift events and I was brought into yet another higher state, which is called the Guru. The Guru transmits or commands a Light called Darshan, which is described as a Divine Blessing. The event itself was intense to say the least. Light flooded through me in a way I had never experienced previously, and to the degree that it was quite alarming. On the one hand I knew what was happening and allowed the Light to flood me, but on the other, the natural 'fear of change' within all of human consciousness was trying to stop the process. It is quite a humorous situation as two aspects of your own consciousness work against each other. One trying to accept this new gift and the other in total terror of it. Having had a lot of practice over the years with the way Light changes your vibration, I think I managed the process reasonably well.

The term Guru is not some appellation that you attach to your ego, it means 'Teacher, Dispeller of Darkness' and is a sacred term that reflects a very sacred level of attainment. In fact, a great deal of my work from my original awakening had been involved with dissolving or dispelling darkness. The energy of fear within the consciousness of all people presents itself as dark energy. Darkness doesn't necessarily mean something awful, bad or evil. It just means absence of Light. You can't have Light and dark in the same place, like a sheet of paper can't be both black and white at the same time. It is either one or the other. When an Emerald Heart Light Practitioner applies a Light Program to a person, it is usually to dissolve a little cloud of darkness that holds them prisoner in some way. As the darkness dissolves, so it is replaced by Light. The result is a shift in vibration.

Traditionally and historically, people would seek out a guru and sit in their presence to absorb the Light radiating from them. The teacher's Light would assist the spiritual aspirant's vibration to rise, resulting in change and evolution of their consciousness. In modern times, this method of assisting people to evolve is largely becoming redundant as we transit into the Age of Aquarius where everything moves faster because of a higher vibration from the Universe bathing our earth and reality. Vibrational change can come quite quickly or it may take years but the Light of a guru calls and radiates into the world so that the hearts that are ready to let go and transform will find it. Universal Light is always calling to the hearts of everyone. When your heart is ready to feel the call, you will awaken and seek a Teacher, Guru or Carrier of Light.

Stepping into Darshan

I had to test out the theory of whether or not I had actually attained this Guru state and if I could actually transmit the Divine Darshan Blessing. The only way to do this is to road test it. I spoke about it with my colleague Tim Dyson and he organised a Darshan Event in London so that we could find the truth of this suspected advancement. We performed the Darshan in the traditional manner, where helpers assisted and prepared the audience. Once the room was calm and all were ready, I came into the room to perform the Darshan transmission, then left afterwards. I spent quite some time in preparation before and in contemplation afterwards to honour the process.

The only way we can learn about our work and judge it with any accuracy is through the feedback of people who have experienced what the energy or Light does for them. In this first experiment, a number of people did indeed have experiences that they could only describe as like being touched by the Divine. That was what I needed to know in order to understand what I had attracted with this most recent vibrational shift.

I then went on the road with Tim bringing the Darshan event to a number of countries, thinking that this would be my next phase of working with Light. Then after just over a year of these events, I was asked to stop travelling. It seemed that I only needed to prove to myself what I had achieved and that it worked. I was then guided to provide Distant Darshan transmissions. Initially, I offered these once a week, but that proved too intense for my system and I changed it to once a month, which I continue to offer to this day. You can sign up and experience it for yourself by joining my mailing list.

Healing the Earth

During this new period of ascension, I was also guided to begin an Earth Healing Community, which is called Circle of Light.

Members of this group offer their hearts as vessels to bring healing to Mother Earth. We do this four times a year, at the solstices and equinoxes. I flow the Light through the hearts of each member of the community enabling them to engage in very powerful earth healing processes. Each time an individual joins the event, as well as the Light passing through their heart to provide healing to our Mother Earth, the Light assists the person's individual evolutionary process and their vibration rises.

You may recall that I mentioned earlier that the Universe works like a reward system. Each person is rewarded through the way the Light develops their heart each time they engage in the Earth Healing process. It is a lovely way to give back to our Mother Earth, and if we had time in this book, I could tell you more about why she needs the healing.

Each time your consciousness shifts
to a higher vibration,
you see ever more through the illusion
of what we think we are.

8 – Cleansing and Purification of Consciousness

When you work with Light, you know that your work is never finished. There is a deep knowing that somehow you are nearly always at the beginning, with a sense of excitement about what is coming next. In order to progress to the next level though, you must always pass through a vibrational shift. This is often accomplished through deep cleansing and purification at different levels of your being, like your thoughts, words and deeds, plus atoning for the past. In fact, the whole path towards aligning with Universal Laws is about purification of the heart. For example, if your life is full of dark thoughts and deeds how can you expect the Light of a Universal Law to align with you? You are only going to attract the same vibration as that which you radiate.

Keeping Myself Busy

Whilst waiting from 2016, I continued to work with clients and teach evolutionary work through writings to my mailing list and offering Light Programs to those who wanted them. I continued with the monthly Distant Darshans and I organised the quarterly Earth Healing Events with the Community. In addition, there is the regular *Fill Your Heart with Light Program* plus the occasional cleansing of property or land in my role as the Earth Doctor. I have been pouring Light into the Earth and people's hearts for a very long time and the one simple tool to help do this is a Light Program. This enables the individual to receive a Light that opens the deeper consciousness in their heart and raises their vibration, which in turn allows them to see their life more clearly and thus, make changes that align them more easily with the Light of Universal Laws. A Light Program always guarantees a vibrational shift in consciousness, and that is what we desire in order to become more successful at life.

After the insight in the garage that day, many more aspects of my life unlocked themselves and I could see how things had unfolded for me in more detail. You might think to yourself, 'Well, David took a very long time to align with and activate the Law of Attraction,' but that is not the case. I actually attracted many things before the cars but I was so busy helping others with the Light that I hadn't really connected the dots.

You could say that attracting the original form of Light that started my journey of awakening was the beginning of aligning with the Law of Attraction in its full measure. Yet, it began even earlier, when I attracted an amethyst crystal at about 12 years of age that eventually lead me to become a crystal healer and develop one of the biggest crystal businesses in Manchester, United Kingdom, including demonstrating crystal healing on TV. I often wished for a house with crystals on every windowsill. I now live in it. When my mother first visited me in my idyllic country cottage, she said to me, 'Oh, David, this is what you always wanted as a boy.' I attracted it once I was ready to receive it. On a humorous note, I was once in the back of an ambulance with a suspected heart attack when one of the ambulance men called out to the other, 'Come and look at this place, it's fantastic!' They both disappeared into my garden leaving me to live or die.

The cleansing and purification is still a huge part of my personal journey.

Karmic Debts Must Always be Settled

When I attracted Spiritual Light into my life it was to help uplift others but also to help me cleanse and settle my karmic debt of some of the terrible things I had done in previous lives. All karma needs to be atoned for at some point in time. As you serve your debts to humanity and the Divine, this then allows your vibration to rise. The cleansing and purification process was and still is, a huge part of my personal journey.

Each time your consciousness shifts to a higher vibration, you see ever more through the illusion of what we think we are. As I worked with the Darshan Light that came to me in 2016, I could see how I had needed to atone for my karmic debts by offering healing to others in this life. We can all benefit by giving healing or comforting service to others, even if it is only a kind word. It is a wonderful way to become more integrated into the flow of the Universal Laws that govern our time on planet earth. As I was paying off my karmic debt with healing work, the Light was also transforming my consciousness. The darkness that I carried from the past was being dispelled and dissolved and I was being raised up. It was like experiencing the scales of justice coming into balance as the doors to more rewards are being prepared. You are always being prepared to receive something new, but many people are content to sit where they are in life and so they don't reach out to experience their dreams and desires.

Your Journey may be much Easier than Mine
You may not have such a dark past to atone for as I did. You may be ready to fly right from the moment you arrive in this life. Just because it took me some time to see what I had achieved using a Spiritual Light doesn't mean that it will take you that long. Moving into harmony with the Universal Laws can be just a step away. I've been in true harmony with it since the late 1980s when my awakening began, but I was focused on helping others rather than manifesting what I wanted in life. Yet the manifestation process was happening all of the time without me being very aware of it. The Light was serving me as I served others with it. That is actually one of the Universal Laws – As you Uplift others, so you are Uplifted yourself.

I have ridden the Wave of Time, where your consciousness is changing by the minute and you see the world differently each day. I've been on the crest of it since the early 90s. That journey of more than 30 years has filled me with a mass of experience, knowledge and wisdom.

My sole purpose in this life is to help uplift and empower others. That is my life-mission. It uplifts me, even if it can be tough work at times, but I expect I will never change from this path. Uplifting humanity is what I do. It is what I was sent here to do. I was given a massive opportunity to be a better human being than I was last time around, and I took it. When opportunity comes, we either push it aside or embrace it. The embracing part is often challenging, but that is how we grow.

The Law of Reflection.

The Law of Attraction is only one tiny part of aligning with the Light of Universal Laws. There is so much more. It is a great and fascinating journey of learning to be able to feel the way.

When people truly desire to reach for the stars, that is what they will attain.

Whilst ever they choose to limit themselves through fear of taking action, that is what they will attain.

That is the Law of Reflection in action.

The Light of the Universe reflects to you what is in your heart, what you truly desire. When you embody that inner desire, then you will succeed in attracting it. It is only a matter of time. It could be starting for you today. Never give up.

You must change the whole dynamic
of your consciousness…

…to align with
Universal Consciousness…

…or any Law that is
encompassed within it.

9 – Aligning with the Laws

It is not so much about attracting the Law of Attraction but more about aligning yourself with the vibration. Your own vibration aligns with the Universal Vibration that desires to manifest what brings you joy.

All consciousness is structured in vibrational levels. It is just like climbing a ladder from one vibrational step to the next. Each colour in a rainbow has a different vibrational frequency, and in fact, we can't see any of those colours unless they are revealed to us through a prism, like the water droplets of rain. Without the rain, we might never see the beauty of Light that is a rainbow, yet it is there, just beyond our vision. Vibrations of consciousness are just the same. It is not until you experience the shift from one level to another that you truly understand the difference it makes to your life. New doors open for you as you attract things of a similar vibration.

We all have a Divine purpose in life. Whether we know it or not, we are all actually trying to align ourselves with that purpose here on earth. Life on earth is a game that we can't get out of. All the powers in the Universe are constantly trying to guide us to success, but we often just get in the way of the Divine or spiritual guidance by ignoring the feelings in our hearts that are pointing us in the right direction.

The Stream of Plenty

Universal Consciousness creates Universes. The collective consciousness of humanity is very good at creating chaos and misery. Gods think like Gods and humans think like humans. You have to change the whole dynamic of your consciousness in order to align with Universal Consciousness, or any Law that is encompassed within it. When we are aligned, then everything flows like a river. As the Emerald Heart Light was teaching me how the Universe worked, it called this flowing river The Stream of Plenty, you just dip into it and pull out what you desire.

Of course, our consciousness doesn't just advance from its present level to that of attracting the full spectrum of Universal Consciousness in one step. It rises in stages and attracts ever higher vibrational assistance from the whole that is available to us. Each step of vibrational attainment that we can make means that we hold more Light at our core. If you went from zero to fully enlightened in an instant, you would burst into flames, it isn't possible. As your vibration rises in small increments, your whole system must learn how to live in this new vehicle with each shift.

Learning to Feel Your Truth

In order to become aligned with the Law of Attraction, the first step is to learn to feel your own truth in your heart. Nothing else should matter to you. Your life is actually a journey between you and the Universal Consciousness. It is not between you and your husband or wife, partner, boss, family or anyone else for that matter. It is an individual journey. If you are aligned with a partner whose vibration is on a similar frequency and trajectory, then that's great, but if you are not, then already, you are learning lessons about non-alignment.

Too many of us are pushed by our parents; what our society says we should do; our circumstances or just opportunities that others tell us are good for us. We can often feel that we don't want to go that way, but we do because we don't have the courage to say no or follow our own heart's desires. Many of us actually drive ourselves away from aligning with our life-purpose and so we then drive ourselves away from any Law that is trying to uplift and support us. Guess what happens then? Nothing goes our way. We are not in the flow. We are actually going against the flow and life becomes difficult. Difficulty is always telling us that we are not going in the right direction or doing the right thing.

If there is no gratitude, then don't expect the next thing to be offered.

Here are some key things to understand:

1. Change
Nothing changes for you unless your vibration changes. Therefore, look at your life often and change even the smallest thing for the better. Your effort will be rewarded.

2. Universal Consciousness
You need a very clear understanding of Universal Consciousness, the Source, God, or whatever you want to call it. It doesn't matter what you call it as it is just one thing with many names, but it is important that you have a relationship with it.

Universal Consciousness is just an ocean of wisdom that is constantly trying to uplift you. Your job is to be as clear as you can about it. For me, I try to see it working in nature around me and take comfort from how clever all beings are at allowing Universal Consciousness to guide them. Animals, plants, trees, they just be what they are and thrive. Look at the magic that is within everything. Look at the tiniest of creatures, like a flea, and imagine the heart that is beating inside it. That is life and life is sacred, honour it and give thanks.

3. Gratitude
Learn to see how you are blessed by all things around you. Then

constantly give thanks for your life and your opportunities. For example, the opportunity of taking your next breath is the most amazing gift of life from the Universe. Don't take it for granted. Give thanks. That is how simple it is to begin to move your vibration upwards. If there is no gratitude, then don't expect the next thing to be offered. Universal Consciousness reflects your heart's desires. It is a reward system. Give thanks and it thanks you.

Wealth has nothing to do with money!

4. Wealth
Learn to understand that wealth has nothing to do with money. Wealth is a state of being and a state of grace within yourself. Being surrounded by the things that you love adds to this state of grace. Bless yourself with the things that feed you with love. When we pour love into something, then it reflects that love back to us. When we are in the radiance of love, that is pure wealth. When we recognise the wealth and the love and give gratitude for it, then more is given.

These words above are fundamental principles of aligning with Universal Laws. Just take these simple steps and already you will be attracting more of what you want to experience and less of what you don't want. You will be moving towards aligning with the Law of Attraction.

It is the vibration of
the Light in your heart
that must change

in order to raise
your vibration.

10 – Understanding Vibration

If you don't understand what you are trying to attract, then you won't attract it. Therefore, there is a fundamental need to understand the nature of the vibration of consciousness.

Outside of ourselves is Universal Consciousness, the Source, the whole thing, the Ocean of Wisdom, which is constantly trying to help you. Inside of us is our own individual consciousness that resides within the heart. Yes, we may think with our mind and brain in the head, but the truth lies in the heart and it is the vibration of the heart that needs to change in order to attract a different reality. It is the Light within your heart that attracts the Light of a similar vibration from the Stream of Plenty which is the flow of Universal Consciousness, helping you to manifest your desires.

The scale of vibration works like the rainbow that I mentioned earlier. At the lower end of the visible spectrum or vibrations of Light you have the red and below that is the infra-red. At the higher end of the spectrum are the faster vibrations of violet and ultra-violet. The red and violet you can see, but the infra-red and ultra-violet you can't see because your eyes cannot resolve those frequencies or vibrations, but nevertheless, they are still there. They exist but you can't see them as colours. The vibrations of Universal Consciousness are just like the infra-red and ultra-violet, they are there but you can't see them.

Heaven and Hell

Humans are capable of the most horrendous acts of violence and destruction against each other. These happen when the person's heart consciousness vibrates at a very low frequency, red, for example, 'He saw red.' Whilst those who vibrate at the higher vibrational frequencies, violet, find that random acts of kindness and altruistic behaviour are their normal mode of functioning.

There is Light and dark, heaven and hell, good and bad. These are all just descriptions of the opposite ends of the vibrational spectrum of consciousness. Just as the red and violet are the extreme ends of the visible spectrum, the opposite ends of the human consciousness spectrum determine the nature and behaviour of each individual.

Creation and Destruction

Then there is Creation and Destruction, again, both are governed by the conscious vibration of the individual's heart. Those who destroy have a lower vibration than those who create.

Law of Attraction

Where do you think the Law of Attraction sits on the vibrational scale? Well, it actually sits everywhere because it is always active for every single person and it works like a reflection.

• If you are altruistic and creative, you will attract the vibration that reflects who and what you are.

• If you are mean and sadistic then you will attract a vibration that fuels that level of consciousness.

• You will attract the reality that reflects the vibration of your heart.

Based on this description above, you can then work out what your heart is showing you at any moment in time and why.

For example, if you are attracting lack of prosperity or bad luck or the wrong job or the wrong people into your life, you absolutely know where your conscious vibration is.

If you are attracting good fortune, luck, creative, uplifting and fulfilling work and happy and supportive people, again, you know what frequency your heart is radiating into the world.

You can monitor yourself at any moment to see what you are attracting. If you are thinking the wrong thoughts, then change them. If you are doing the wrong things, then change what you are doing. It is about being self-aware. Monitor yourself and get to know your Self. The ancient maxim, which was carved in stone at the Temple of Apollo in Delphi says, 'Know thy Self.'

At any moment in time, the Universal Consciousness is reflecting your own vibration or truth to you. If you wish to change that truth you can. We are all the masters of our own destinies. Anyone who works hard to change themselves is immediately supported and rewarded by the Universe. It can't not support you for it is automatically reflecting what is in your heart all the time.

What do People Aspire to Attract?
Most people have never heard of Universal Laws or the Law of Attraction in particular, so they have no idea that they can actually influence change in their lives by consciously changing their vibration. Not only that but if your vibration changes, then you radiate more light into the world. Those who are close to you will benefit and their own vibration may even rise as a result of yours rising. If everyone's vibration raised by one degree, the whole of humanity would change for the better.

If your vibration rose suddenly and dramatically, how do you think that would affect you? Do you think, for example, that you would attract material wealth with it? Of course you wouldn't, because your thinking would be closer to the Divine and thus, more altruistic. You would look at the suffering of humanity and try to help people to heal. Money is a very narrow focus and who does it serve? It could be said that trying to attract money for personal prosperity is a very selfish focus. If you look at those people who chase that kind of wealth, nothing is enough, there is always something else that is wanted or needed in order to sate the appetite for more.

We are just the Bridge between two Worlds.

When you do the work on yourself, then the money comes. It doesn't work the other way around. For example, when I was training healers many moons ago, I helped a woman out of a very dark place and pointed her in the right direction to start her healing practice. About a year later, she got in touch to say that she was in a bad place again and needed help. I asked her what happened to her healing aspirations and she told me that she had been praying and asking for the money so that she could start work. 'Stop right there,' I said. 'That is not how it works.'

You do the work and then the money comes. She told me that she didn't have anywhere to offer healing. I mentioned that the only place you need is in your heart. If someone tells you their troubles and they are ready to be helped, then help them. Just sit with them and allow the Universe to work through you in that moment. Sit on a park bench and do it. No matter what the circumstances, just do it. We don't make excuses for not doing the work.

One day quite recently, I was visiting a garage and the car painter, who had lost a leg and was in a wheelchair, had recently had a stroke to add to his misery, but he was still joyful in his work. I asked him would he like some healing and he said yes, so in the middle of the garage on a working day with the doors wide open on to the street, I gave him healing. It is that simple. It is about allowing the Universe to work through us to help others. Take this book for example. The Universe is guiding me to write it so that it helps you to find the Light that can raise your vibration and bring change to your life. This book is just another form of healing, another way to bring Light to the world. The Light in the words alone will help you. The more you read it, the more it will reveal to you as your vibration rises. Life is all about healing the things that hold us back.

When the heart is developed with Light, we become a bridge between worlds. When there is need and a desire to receive, then Light will flow from the source, through the healer to the needy. We just open ourselves to allow it to happen.

If you had the ability to make thousands of lives better, how do you think the heart consciousness would feel about that? How do you think Universal Consciousness would feel about that? Everything would flow for you and whatever you need to do your work would come.

I never have a lot of money, but I have everything that I need and when I need more, the money comes. I am wealthy beyond measure. I work with energy and Light and money is just an energy. If you can create the flow, it comes to you as you need it. On a humorous note, not many years ago my mother, in a moment of exasperation said to me, 'Oh David, you've had so much money through your hands, why have you never got any?' I laughed and replied, 'Because it just flows Mum.' The trick is to keep it flowing.

As Rumi once said:

'Go to the market place and buy something, just to be part of the exchange.'

Rumi, in this quote, is explaining the nature of creating a flow. Everything in the Universe works by exchange and exchange creates flow. There has to be flow and there has to be exchange, otherwise, nothing works. The only way you can create flow is by not holding on to anything, but allowing it to flow. Take note when something doesn't serve you or bring you joy any longer, then let it go. Don't hoard things or the energy in them becomes useless and dead. Dead energy is heavy and it slows your vibration and your ability to attract new things.

When you make an investment in something like healing or the evolution of your consciousness, how do you think Universal Consciousness reflects upon that exchange? As the Universe is always trying to offer assistance, it takes this amazing opportunity to uplift you *via* the exchange.

I recall many years ago sitting at my desk one morning and feeling amazed at the spiritual abilities that had developed within me. I said to myself, 'I have so many incredible abilities that I couldn't possibly want for anything else.' Shortly afterwards, I attracted The Emerald Heart Light, which again brought me more than I could ever have imagined in the development of my heart.

The Key to Success

The key to attracting more of the good stuff is through self-reflection. Keep looking at your Self, your behaviour. Analyse the good things that you are and do and also analyse and reflect upon the bad things that you are and do. List them all down in a journal, and keep working with it. When you write it down and reflect upon it, you move that energy out of yourself and onto a page. The energy becomes totally different. Once that energy is out of your Self, then you become freer, lighter and your vibration will respond to that.

The basic marker to help you change your vibration is understanding your Self and your motivations, your driving forces. Are you selfish, self-centred, self-oriented, self-possessed, or are you open, available, altruistic, generous? Are you a giver or a taker? What do you wish to change about your Self? Write it down and ask for Divine Guidance to help you. It works.

Universal Consciousness will help you. If you have acquired this book for example, you have already sent a message to the Universe that you want to develop yourself. It will reflect your desire to you through opportunities to see and take. As you respond differently to situations, your vibration rises. Remind yourself of that corny old saying, 'If you keep doing what you have always been doing, then you'll keep getting what you've always been getting.' Trite, it may be, but true it is.

Where Does Universal Consciousness Vibrate?

We could say for arguments sake that Universal Consciousness is the highest point of the vibrational spectrum of consciousness. Universal Consciousness is creating creation, creating universes and creating worlds. All it does, is create all of the time. When people speak about The Creator, they are often unknowingly referring to a vibration that they have applied a personality to. Universal Consciousness is like an ocean of wisdom that is available to everyone. We are swimming in it all of the time, but in order to attract it in a way that manifests for you, you have to keep working at raising your vibration until you arrive at a similar frequency to that which you wish to attract. Like, for example, the cars that I had a love for.

Of course, there are many levels of vibration on the scale below the ultimate one and if you use the rainbow idea as a guide, you are always heading towards a higher vibration, which is the violet, then moving beyond that into the ultra-violet. Then your next target is even higher than that.

The key to measuring where you are is how you feel in your heart, how open your heart is and what touches your heart. For example, if you walk through a field of flowers and don't even see or smell them, your vibration is low, but if you are struck by the beauty of what lies in front of you, then you know that you are receiving the vibration that they radiate by being in alignment with their high vibration. 'Stop and smell the roses,' is a well-known saying, but people don't realise the spiritual message in it. When you 'allow' your Self to stop and smell the roses, or any other flower for that matter, then you allow the Universe to work through the flower and bring you something uplifting that may well assist your vibration to rise. Most of our common sayings are actually instructions in how to raise your vibration. When you are thankful and grateful for the experience the rose gives you, the Universe offers you more things of that frequency so that you can experience even more of that love.

By slowing your life down and being more aware, you will allow your heart time to feel the truth of any situation. As your heart learns how to feel the truth at a deeper level, you become more aligned with higher vibrations.

Spiritual Light is a Key that can Change your Vibration

I have been bringing Light into the world for more than 30 years, helping people to move beyond what limits them. This is done by targeting certain dark energies within them with Light and dissolving those energies out of their consciousness. We all carry fears and fears are like little clouds of dark energy that float around inside you. If you can dissolve even just an ounce of dark energy from your consciousness, that darkness is replaced by Light. There is no vacuum, there is only Light and dark. For each ounce of darkness that is dissolved, a person carries an additional ounce of Light. Each ounce of additional Light raises your vibration. Simple!

If you constantly find yourself in the presence of people or situations that pull you down, then change the pattern of being in that situation. Be with people who uplift you. Attract new friends.

Evolution of Human Consciousness can only go one way, which is up. Humans can't do de-volution as the natural laws are always moving us higher. All we have to do is keep looking at ourselves and seeing what needs to change in our thoughts, words, deeds and actions and that will help to raise our vibration.

Why would the Laws be given to us,

if we were not ready to learn
how to align with them?

11 – An Overview of Now

The consciousness of humanity is diamond bright, but it can easily become tainted by circumstances and difficulties. Let's face it, life on earth can be tough at times.

Make an Effort

Over the years, I have found that I must make an effort to pull myself out of the patterns, influences and dramas of everyday life and try and see the bigger picture. We are here for a very short time, but in that time, we have a massive opportunity to align ourselves with our divine purpose, of which we all have one. If we do nothing to change, then the next life will be much the same as this one. We will return in the same vibration as our present life and that is not a good plan.

Attracting the Light of Growth and Change

There is more than enough evidence these days for the continuing process of life on the other side of this reality. When you begin to align yourself with this bigger picture, the fact that life doesn't cease but merely transforms from one state to another and back again, then your consciousness is already expanding and your vibration rising. You can ask yourself, 'how can I play my part in developing my own growth and raising my vibration?' As your vibration rises, this in turn helps others, which in turn helps humanity to grow and prosper as a whole? As you embrace this idea, then your consciousness opens and expands. In the process of expansion, the Light that is behind the whole of creation will flow towards you. You will attract it. It will help you!

Universal consciousness is always evolving. It never sleeps and as our world is bathed in this Light, we are forced into expansion and growth. Evolution of consciousness equals the raising of vibration. We are all engaged in a process of evolution of consciousness whether we realise it or not. The Emerald Heart Light and the Laws that were given with it, taught me that this Light is an accelerator and expander of consciousness. As you invest in it and drink it in to your heart, it nurtures your aspirations and desires. You develop, grow and prosper.

The success of our earth-bound reality is based upon the vibration of consciousness that we can hold collectively as a species. If we can continually raise our vibration, then our reality constantly changes. As each individual works upon themselves, the vibrational waves that emanate from them influences the growth of others. Everything we do to raise our own vibration is assisted by the Universe too, which, as I have explained, is the Law of Reflection in action.

We inhabit a beautiful jewel in the darkness of space. The planet of Light. Take a look at those photographs that the first astronauts took of the earth and you will see this glowing jewel. We are like atoms that are part of this beautiful jewel. The more that we can entrain our consciousness into expansion, the more we connect with and feel a part of this jewel and its life-force. The more we are connected, then the more we attract good things towards ourselves.

The Laws of the Universe have been given to guide us into the opportunities that await us if we will only invest some time, energy and Light into our lives. We all have an opportunity to help ourselves and others raise their vibration by learning to see things in a new way, prospering as a result and radiating a new or different vision of reality into the world from our hearts.

We are not separate. We are a living part of a great game, a game that encompasses the whole Universe. Everything we think or do ripples throughout that great continuum. If we play the game by the Laws, then we all prosper. If we think we have no chance, then that is the vibration that we will radiate into our reality and then 'no chance' is the vibration that will reflect back to us. Which do you want?

Everything must flow otherwise it becomes stagnant. As I work with the Emerald Heart Light, I am fully aware that it is a Light for the Evolution of Human Consciousness and because if this, the Light itself constantly evolves and changes. Those of us who work with it closely must constantly address our lives and change things for the better, otherwise the Light will leave us behind. The Light is always trying to expand and bring itself into the world. It is a living being offering itself to everyone so they can be uplifted and benefit. It is always there, waiting for you to see it and wanting it to bless your life.

The Key to Success is in your Heart

At this point, I would bring you back to the vision that human consciousness has this brilliant, diamond-like quality that can shine into the world and illuminate the goodness that is within everyone's heart. We all have a Light at our core, but what can we do to illuminate it to the next level? How do we turn a glow into a blazing sun? For example, people may concentrate on eating good food for their body, or working hard to develop their mind, but what percentage of humanity actually works to develop the consciousness within their heart? I can tell you that it is a tiny, fraction of a percentage, yet bringing Light into your heart is the key to the success of the individual and the species as a whole.

As I work with people, they tell me how they can see or feel the Light flowing out of me and into them. When I transmit Darshan once a month, the feedback I receive shows me how people experience the Light. My Divine purpose is to learn how to bring this Light into the world so that people like you can grow and prosper. In this book, I am showing you where and how you can access the Light and bring it into your own heart. The rest is really up to you.

As our reality is progressing through evolutionary change as Universal Consciousness speeds up, humans will have no choice as to whether they develop their consciousness or not. They will be pushed into change, or pushed off the planet. Why wait to be pushed, when there is a Light here already that is preparing people to be the leaders of a new reality, doing good things for our world by uplifting the vibration of the people. All of us are carriers of Light. The Emerald Heart Light, awakens and empowers our own Light and guides us into becoming who we came here to be.

The Emerald Heart Light is a Light that guides us towards our divine right to wealth and prosperity. It is the Light of Love.

The Law of Attraction is basically The Law of Love.

Like attracts like. What you love will be attracted to you.

The whole game of life is predicated upon Love. As soon as you understand this and move towards it, then Love moves towards you.

PART 2

HOW TO ACCESS THE LIGHT
FOR YOURSELF

An Emerald Heart Light Program

always GUARANTEES

a shift in vibration.

12 – What are the Benefits to You?

The benefits are really incalculable. The whole journey of humanity is to become deeply connected with your heart, and then the heart of the Universe. As mentioned previously, we are all connected heart to heart in a matrix. When you can see or feel this connection, it changes your whole perspective on why we are here. The Emerald Heart Light moves you ever closer to the depth of this reality. Since I brought the Light and the Teachings into our world, thousands of people have received a Light Program, many of them returning time after time over many years.

Universal Consciousness works directly through the Light with your own higher-self in your heart. Your life-journey is really between your heart and the highest form of Universal Consciousness. The Light focuses and helps you as the individual you are. But in general terms it can help you with the following:

- Helping you with healing
- Opening your heart
- Removing blockages to your life
- Developing your potential
- Revealing your hidden gifts and talents
- Expanding your awareness
- Broadening your horizons
- Helping you see the truth of who you are
- Guiding you to see the changes you need to make

- Illuminating the things that block you
- Aligning you with the Universal Laws.
- Aligning you with Universal Consciousness
- Attracts the things you need to see and experience for your growth

Or, indeed, the Light may just offer you support in whatever way is the best for you in the moment. Whatever an Emerald Heart Light Program may be helping you with, there is always one divine focus, which will raise your vibration.

Finally, an Emerald Heart Light Program always guarantees a shift in vibration and is offered with a 100% money back guarantee, no questions asked.

Request a Connection

to the

Emerald Heart Light!

13 – Access the Emerald Heart Light here!

www.Law-of-Attraction.guru

Once in the website:

Go to the Register of Connections

Have a look at the Register of Connections. You will see the first name of the person and their location in the world is listed. The Register began in 2005.

Request a Connection to the Light

Follow the simple instructions to receive a connection to the Light. The Connection is called an **Emerald Heart Light Program**.

The Connection is Instant

Once connected, which is instant, the Light will be poured gently into your heart for 28 days. It then unfolds within you for around 12 weeks. Some people even feel the Light before completing the registration.

Check Your Connection

Your name will appear in the Register of Connections usually within a day of your request.

The Light always guarantees a shift in vibration.

- Sometimes the shift is monumental and you have no doubt you have experienced it.

- Sometimes, it is less intense, but still moving you in the right direction.

- Sometimes the shift creeps up on you some weeks or even months later. You wake up one morning absolutely 'knowing' that something has changed. You can never tell what it is, but you start to see things differently and have an absolute inner knowing that it's happened.

- Other people may feel the change within you before you do. They will often ask, 'What is different about you?'

- You can request up to five Emerald Heart Light Programs in a year, which is roughly one every ten weeks. This will keep you in the Light for a whole year.

- The vibrational shifts are cumulative with each Light Program. You are always moving forwards and your vibration is always rising.

Additional ways
that you can

Access the Light

for your own growth
and development.

14 – More Ways to Access the Light

Mailing List

www.Law-of-Attraction.guru

By signing up to my mailing list you will be informed whenever any event or Light Program is being offered. You will receive regular spiritual teachings and guidance too.

Darshan Blessing

www.davidashworth.guru

You may wish to join my regular Distant Darshan Blessing. The Blessing is transmitted at a distance so that you can receive it wherever you are, at your leisure and within your own comfortable space.

Focused Formulas and other Light Programs

Monthly transmissions of Light which are focused in a particular way to help carry you through life and get the best from it.

Evolutionary Alignment Programs

Programs that align you with the Universal Vibrations of the moment.

Fill Your Heart with Light Essence Programs

Regular Programs or Light transmissions to help with healing, support, spiritual growth and transformation.

Circle of Light Earth Healing Community
Take part in our World-wide Earth Healing Events four times a year on the Solstices and Equinoxes, where Light is poured through your heart and into Mother Earth. Both you and Mother Earth benefit from the Light.

Emerald Heart School of Enlightenment
www.emerald-heart.com
David founded the School in 2005.
Sign up to the blog to keep informed of all events offered by Emerald Heart Light Teachers, Practitioners and Healers or contact the above if you would like personal help with anything.

Books
David has written a number of books about the spiritual journey and how to walk such a path with success. Books are available through the websites.

Around 7 to 8 weeks

into the Light Program

you start to go through

a vibrational shift.

GUARANTEED!

15 – How does the Light Work?

A connection to the Light is called an Emerald Heart Light Program. In simple terms this connection acts like pouring a bowl full of beautiful evolutionary divine Light into your heart. As the Light is poured in, then your own higher-consciousness begins to use it for your own healing and development.

The Light comes to you directly from the Source of all Light, which is Universal Consciousness. It works with you the moment you register, even before your name appears on the Register of Connections. Although the feelings and experiences may vary and be different for many people, below is a guide in the way that it tends to work.

1. Once you initiate your connection, the Light flows gently into your heart for 28 days. Right from the beginning, your own higher-self focuses the Light on any issues or difficulties that hold your life back from its divine development. The Light Program works to clear anything that blocks you. The Light will attempt to guide you towards anything that is not in alignment with your best interests or divine life purpose. In the removal of these energies that block you, your vibration eventually rises.

2. The Light creates movement and illumination in your higher-self, which is in your heart. The Light will seek out and dissolve any energies that prevent your consciousness from unfolding and evolving.

3. Around 7 to 8 weeks into the Light Program you start to go through a vibrational shift. This can be sudden and you feel it clearly, or it can be gentle and then you begin to notice that something is different about you as the weeks unfold. An Emerald Heart Light Program absolutely guarantees a vibrational shift at some level. As myself and my colleagues have worked with this Light since 2005, we have a vast experience of how it helps in all manner of situations through the mental, emotional, spiritual and physical dimensions of our being.

4. As your vibration rises, the Light continues to guide your consciousness towards awakening you to anything that needs to change, in both your inner and outer worlds. As the Program completes between week 8 and 12, the Light brings you into the balance of your newly raised vibrational state.

The Universe will always try to help you see that you have changed. A very common way of knowing this comes to you from outside. Other people often ask 'What is different about you?' They often notice the changes before we do ourselves because we radiate a different vibration into the world. Others pick this up sub-consciously. Also, you often feel much Lighter and freer than before with a renewed enthusiasm for life.

Journaling
It is a good idea to keep a little journal to note down anything out of the ordinary that happens to you whilst drinking in the Light of your Program. Universal Consciousness always tries to let you know that you are in the Light and that it is working for you, so note down anything out of the ordinary that happens in your life.

Fear of Change

holds most

human beings back

16 – Asking the Light to Help You

When Requesting a Connection for an Emerald Heart Light Program, you can accept the Light just as it is and it will work for your own highest good on the energies that most limit the evolution of your consciousness. Or, you can ask the Light of the Program to help you with anything specific.

When we ask for specific help, we call this a Target. You can ask the Light to aim itself at a target. Imagine shooting an arrow from a bow into a target. When the Light was first teaching me how to dissolve dark energy within people, it would show me the image of shooting an arrow from a bow into a target. The Light would say, 'Don't just aim for the target. Aim for the very centre of the target. Now fire your arrow of Light into the Fear that you want to dissolve.'

All you need to do is write your 'Target' on a piece of paper and put it in a sacred place, somewhere that you might keep your favourite or sacred things. You can create a little altar with crystals, feathers or anything that appeals to your sensitivities for example.

The Darkness that holds us back
Almost every human being struggles with certain energies in life. We may all be debilitated by any number of everyday issues or fears at some level, even at a sub-conscious level.

Here are some examples of everyday Issues and Fears

Lack of Inner Strength
Lack of Direction in Life
Lack of Focus
Inability to make decisions

Fear of Being Different
Fear of Change
Fear of What Others May Think
Fear of Being Judged

As mentioned previously, the energy of fear is dark energy and if you can dissolve this out of your system it is replaced with Light, as there cannot be a vacuum. There can only be Light or darkness. As the darkness is replaced by Light, then your vibration rises and evolution takes place, often accompanied by a clear shift in the way you see your life and your place in the world.

A fear is always the foundation beneath an issue, so if you can identify any of your inner fears, you can then Target them with the Emerald Heart Light Program and it will help to dissolve them.

Collective Consciousness Fears

An example of a fear that is prevalent in the collective consciousness of humanity and therefore affects almost everyone at some level, is Fear of Change. The ego structure doesn't like anything to change because lack of change offers inner security.

Here is a list of Common Issues and Fears to help you

The following Issues and Fears are offered as a guide to help you find a 'Target Issue' when choosing your Emerald Heart Light Program. Some items appear in more than one category, as there may be different underlying reasons. You don't have to choose a target as the Light will help you without one, but it is an option if you feel you need specific help with a certain issue or fear.

If you wish to use a Target, use your Self-knowledge, Feelings, Inner Guidance, Intuition, Dowsing or Muscle Testing to help you find any specific problem areas that you need help with.

Some Common Issues

Lack of Self-worth
Lack of Self-belief
Lack of Clarity
Lack of Inner Strength
Lack of Vision and Perception
Lack of Direction in Life
Lack of Trust in Your Self
Lack of Trust in your Own Judgement
Lack of Trust in your Feelings
Inability to Let Go and Surrender to Inner Guidance
Self-abandonment
Self-denial
Unworthiness
Poverty Consciousness
Lack of Grounding
Clarity of Purpose

Issues are always underpinned by a fear. You need to get down to and dissolve the energy of the fear in order to free yourself from the issue.

Some Common Spiritual Fears

Fear of Change
Fear of Evolution (unlocking of inner self)
Fear of Walking the Right Path
Fear of Being Right/Wrong
Fear of Standing Alone in the World
Fear of Reality
Fear of Flying (evolutionary)
Fear of Listening to/or hearing the Truth

Fear of Light
Fear of Power
Fear of Touching God
Fear of Being Seen/Watched by God
Fear of the Unknown
Fear of My Own Intuition
Fear of Being Free
Fear of Getting it Wrong
Fear of Being Different
Fear of Spiritual Enlightenment
Fear of What you Might Find

Fears around Evolution of Consciousness and Moving Forward
Fear of Standing out in a Crowd
Fear of Letting others Down
Fear of Trying
Fear of Failure
Fear of Being Successful/of Success
Fear of Moving Forward
Fear of not Being Strong Enough
Fear of Leaving Home
Fear of the Outside
Fear of Being Out of My Depth
Fear of Change
Fear of Being Left Behind
Fear of Being Overwhelmed (by life/by others)
Fear of Abandonment
Fear of Being Alone
Fear of Being in Control
Fear of Being Out of Control
Fear of Ego
Fear of Looking a Fool
Fear of Making a Mistake
Fear of Accepting Truth
Fear of Being Different

Fear of Being Left Behind
Fear of Being Undermined/Ridiculed
Fear of Being Complete
Fear of Trusting My Own Judgement
Fear of Being too Successful
Fear of Letting Go
Fear of Being in one Place too Long
Fear of Asking for Help
Lack of Confidence
Abandonment
Unworthy of Being Heard
Unworthiness
Confusion/Lack of Direction
Lack of Happiness
Lack of Inner Strength
Inability to Achieve
Inability to Cope

Fears of the Self

Fear of Being Me/Myself
Fear of My Own Power/Standing in own Power
Fear of My Own Ability
Fear of Trusting
Fear of Not Being Good Enough (to be here)
(to achieve what I want)
Fear of Doing the Right Thing
Fear of Loving Myself
Fear of Femininity/Being Feminine
Fear of Masculinity/Being Masculine
Fear of Close Relationships
Fear of Knowing Who I Am
Fear of Who I Am
Fear of Being Lonely/Unsupported
Fear of Looking Inward
Fear of Life

Fear of Reality
Fear of Death
Fear of Sex/Sexual Repression
Fear of Letting Anyone get too Close
Fear of Identity
Fear of Being Hurt
Fear of Giving Myself to others
Fear of Enjoying Myself (guilt)
Fear of Loving Yourself
Fear of Loneliness
Fear of My Own Sexuality
Fear of Blindness (blind with rage)
Fear of Walking the Wrong Path
Fear of Being Successful
Fear of My Own Inner-Self
Fear of My Own Self
Fear of Looking at/Being Myself
Fear of Looking into My Own Heart
Fear of Not Being Good Enough – Sexually
Fear of Men/Women
Fear of Being Like my Father/Mother

Feeling Lost/Alone
Lack of Identity
Inability to see Yourself
Who Am I?
Disconnection from your Self (separation)
Lack of Self-Love (poor me)
Self-Hatred
Loss of Personal Identity

What on Earth is Going on in my Life?
Lack of Trust/
Lack of Self-Belief
Ignoring your Inner/Own Needs

Unable to Hear Him/Herself
Unworthiness
Self-Sabotage
Desperation

Past Life and Primordial Fears
Fear of Incarnation
Fear of Terror/Terror of Responsibility
Fear of Past Lives/Touching the Past/Reincarnation
Fear of Repeating Mistakes of the Past
Fear of the Unexpected
Fear of Eternity
Fear of Being Trapped
Fear of Running (away or to something/or yourself)
Fear of Unhealed Pain and Issues
Fear of Being Eaten Alive
Fear of Whole Life Falling Apart
Fear of Not Being Good Enough to be on Earth

You become the Light

And the Light

Becomes You!

17 – The End is Just the Beginning

As I mentioned at the beginning, this book is not about teaching you the Law of Attraction. It is about showing where and how you can access the Light that changed my life and helped me attract the things that I love.

I can't put 30 plus years of healing and spiritual teaching experience into this little book, but I will offer more lessons to help you find your way. Join my mailing list to keep informed.

Once you have been connected to an Emerald Heart Light Program, your heart recognises it and will let you know if and when you may benefit from another Light Program. The Light is always calling to the hearts of humanity to offer its help. There are those who have worked with Light Programs for years and they automatically know when they need to drink from the cup again, as they learn to feel the call in their heart.

How often can I have a Connection to the Light?
You can take up to 5 Emerald Heart Light Programs a year, that's one about every 10 weeks. You may be able to take other Programs that are offered through our mailing list at certain times of the year and you can also receive the monthly Darshan Light Blessing or join the Earth Healing events. All of these things will help your vibration to rise.

A Note About the Emerald Heart Light

You can't know the Light – You just have to TRUST it. It comes to you through TRUST. Allow it to call to your heart. Your heart will know the truth of it. Once you feel it in your heart, don't allow your mind to divert you from what your heart feels. That is how people regularly walk away from the Law of Attraction. The mind has its own agenda, but your heart knows the truth.

The Law of Balance in Exchange

Some of you will ask why there is an exchange to be made for the Light.

- Is the Light not freely available from the Universe? Yes!
- Is it not available from the Universe to everyone? Yes!

You can access it from the Universe and bring it into your heart just as I did. Once you have aligned with it in some way, then you will attract it. Until then, you can use Emerald Heart Light Programs to assist you.

There is nothing wrong with asking this question about the exchange and why it is. With time, experience, knowledge and wisdom you will understand the answer. Essentially, the Light is governed by Universal Laws and there is always an exchange needed in order to attract a flow. You could even say it is a process of give and take.

As you learn how to value an exchange at the appropriate level, then all will flow to you. I am not going to teach you these Laws here. You will learn how to align with them as you go along. As your vibration rises and you hold more light, you eventually become the Light itself.

You become the Light and the Light becomes you!

The Light will cost you less than the price of a cup of coffee a day... and may bring you ten-fold that amount in return - (Laws again). It's all to do with the Light and truth in your own heart and how deeply you desire the Light to be with you.

Examples of the Law of Balance in Exchange
Here are a couple of examples of how we are given life through the Law of Balance in Exchange.

Trees exchange carbon dioxide for oxygen, which allows us to breathe. We exchange oxygen for carbon dioxide, which enables the trees to breathe. We are dependent upon each other.

The sun exchanges hydrogen for helium in a fusion process that produces light and heat. This allows all things on our planet to live, grow and thrive, including ourselves. Without the sun, all things die. Spiritual Light is the consciousness behind all things that live, grow and thrive.

That's all there is to it.

- Go to the website - www.Law-of-Attraction.guru
- Do some research and check me out, I've been teaching for a very long time
- Look at the Register of Connections
- Join the mailing list and get updates on what's on offer
- Allow the Light to touch your heart and you will know what to do

With my Deepest Love and Blessings,

David.

The End...

...is Just the Beginning!

Printed in Poland
by Amazon Fulfillment
Poland Sp. z o.o., Wrocław
21 July 2023

03b847e2-d094-45f3-9dbd-76fcece820cfR01